Science

YEAR 6

Answers

Sue Hunter

Jenny Macdonald

GALORE PARK

AN HACHETTE UK COMPANY

Although every effort has been made to ensure that website addresses are correct at time of going to press, Galore Park cannot be held responsible for the content of any website mentioned in this book. It is sometimes possible to find a relocated web page by typing in the address of the home page for a website in the URL window of your browser.

Hachette UK's policy is to use papers that are natural, renewable and recyclable products and made from wood grown in sustainable forests. The logging and manufacturing processes are expected to conform to the environmental regulations of the country of origin.

Orders: please contact Bookpoint Ltd, 130 Milton Park, Abingdon, Oxon OX14 4SB. Telephone: +44 (0)1235 827827. Lines are open 9.00a.m.–5.00p.m., Monday to Saturday, with a 24-hour message answering service. Visit our website at www.galorepark.co.uk for details of other revision guides for Common Entrance, examination papers and Galore Park publications.

Published by Galore Park Publishing Ltd

An Hachette UK company

Carmelite House

50 Victoria Embankment

London EC4Y 0DZ

www.galorepark.co.uk

Text copyright © Sue Hunter and Jenny Macdonald 2015

Impression number 10 9 8 7 6 5 4 3 2 1

2019 2018 2017 2016 2015

Typeset in India

Printed in the UK by Hobbs the Printers Ltd, Totton, Hampshire, SO40 3WX

Illustrations by Integra software services Pvt. Ltd

A catalogue record for this title is available from the British Library.

ISBN: 9781471847585

About the authors

Sue Hunter has been a science teacher in a variety of schools for more years than she cares to remember. Her experiences have included teaching in a choir school and a local authority middle school, teaching GCSE and A level in the Netherlands and a short spell as a full-time mother of two. She was Head of Science at St Hugh's School in Oxfordshire until her recent retirement and is a member of the Common Entrance setting team. She has run a number of training courses for prep school teachers, including at Malvern College and for the Independent Association of Preparatory Schools (IAPS), and is currently IAPS Subject Leader for science and a member of the Independent Schools Inspectorate. She has also served for a number of years as a governor of local primary schools.

Jenny Macdonald has been a teacher for many years, teaching in both state and private schools. For the last 15 years she has been teaching science at St Hugh's School in Oxfordshire. She moved to Oxfordshire in the 1970s and has always enjoyed outdoor pursuits, having raised three children and countless chickens, sheep and dogs on the family small holding. She is chairman of a local choral society, sings in a variety of local choirs, and would like to have more time to relax in the chairs that she enjoys re-upholstering.

Contents

Introduction

About this book

Science is a subject that invites enquiry. The text in *Science Year 6* contains many interesting facts and opens the way for further research should a child feel inclined to find out more. Each chapter includes a number of exercises that are designed to focus the readers' attention on what they have read, assess their understanding of the material and to encourage them to think more analytically about the topic. There are a number of different types of exercise, e.g. cloze ('fill in the gaps') exercises, comprehension type questions and extension exercises requiring thought and application. All can be used in a number of ways depending on the ability of the pupils and the requirements of a lesson. The extension exercises, for example, could be used by teachers as stimuli for discussion, homework activities, opportunities for further development for quick workers, etc.

The answers given here should be seen as a guide. We do not expect every child to reproduce our answers exactly and each child should be encouraged to respond to the best of their ability. For some, success will be achieved if they can correctly extract basic information from the text. Others can be encouraged to look for more than the most basic answer by reading the text more critically. Those with the ability and interest can be encouraged to find out more and expand their knowledge through further reading or to think more deeply about the implications and applications of the material offered.

Sue Hunter and Jenny Macdonald
June 2015

Classification and keys

This chapter covers the following elements of the National Curriculum for Year 6.

Pupils should be taught to:

- describe how living things are classified into broad groups according to common observable characteristics and based on similarities and differences, including micro-organisms, plants and animals
- give reasons for classifying plants and animals, based on specific characteristics.

Notes and guidance:

- Pupils might work scientifically by: using classification systems and keys to identify some animals and plants in the immediate environment.

It also includes the following elements not mentioned in the National Curriculum:

- distinction between features that are diagnostic and those that are not (ISEB Y6 1b)
- how to make an identification key (ISEB Y6 1a).

Activities in this chapter offer opportunities to work scientifically by:

- making careful observations
- distinguishing between diagnostic and non-diagnostic features of organisms
- using observed characteristics and a key to identify or classify an organism
- making a key using observed diagnostic characteristics.

Exercise 1.1a

1 They all have a backbone/internal bony skeleton.
2 mammals and birds
3 Mammals have fur to insulate their bodies, marine mammals have fat/blubber. Birds have feathers. (They all convert energy from food into heat to warm their bodies.)
4 Body temperature matches the temperature of the environment. Unable to warm their bodies internally.
5 fish, reptiles and amphibians
6 Usually by basking in sunlight.
7 mammals, birds, adult amphibians, reptiles
8 mammals
9 Wings have become adapted to be like flippers to propel them through the water.

Exercise 1.1b

1 characteristics

2 backbone

3 reptiles, amphibians, mammals

4 gills

5 lungs

6 fur, milk

Exercise 1.1c: extension

Reptiles and amphibians	
Similarities	Differences
They both have four legs.	Young amphibians are tadpoles, but young reptiles look like their parents.
They both lay eggs.	Amphibians lay eggs in water, but reptiles lay them on land.
They are both cold-blooded.	Amphibian eggs are surrounded by jelly, but reptile eggs have leathery shells.
Both breathe through lungs (although young amphibians have gills).	Reptiles have dry scaly skin, but amphibians have smoother moist skins.

Other observations may be included.

Exercise 1.2a

1 Vertebrates have a backbone/internal bony skeleton but invertebrates do not.

2 A hard casing round the outside of the animal's body, made from chitin.

3 allow any arthropod

4 Snails are able to pull the soft parts of their bodies back into their shell if threatened by a predator.

5 head, thorax and abdomen

6 Insects have three parts to their bodies, three pairs of legs and most have wings. Spiders have two parts to their bodies, four pairs of legs and no wings.

7 Insects pollinate many types of plant so they develop fruits and seeds.

Exercise 1.2b

1 invertebrates

2 insects

3 colony

4 three, six

5 two, eight

6 bite, web

Exercise 1.3

1 There are so many different types of organism that it is much easier to study them and make sense of observations if they are grouped together.

2 Different people studying the same organisms gave them different names.

3 Swedish

4 A system that made it easier for scientists all around the world to share their findings and communicate effectively about the organisms they were studying.

5 structure of plant, leaf shape and flower structure

6 all over Europe

7 Each organism has a two part Latin name, the genus name, which identifies the small group to which it belongs, and the species name, making a combination that is unique to that organism.

8 *Equus caballus* (the genus name always has a capital letter but the species name always starts with a lower case letter).

Exercise 1.4: extension

This will need to be individually assessed. Give credit for the use of diagnostic features and organisation of the key as well as whether it can be successfully used to identify individuals.

Exercise 1.5a

1 (a) earwig

  (b) ground beetle

  (c) harvestman

  (d) mite

2 Does the animal have its legs sticking out of the sides of its body? (Accept valid alternatives.)

3 (a) fallow deer

  (b) fox

  (c) badger

  (d) pony

  (e) sheep

  (f) pet cat

Exercise 1.5b: extension

Pupils should be able to sort a range of animals and plants into the correct taxonomic groups and be able to mention at least one distinguishing characteristic used to classify each organism.

2 Healthy living

This chapter covers the following elements of the National Curriculum for Year 6.

Pupils should be taught to:

- identify and name the main parts of the human circulatory system, and describe the functions of the heart, blood vessels and blood
- recognise the impact of diet, exercise, drugs and lifestyle on the way their bodies function
- describe the ways in which nutrients and water are transported within animals, including humans.

It also includes the following elements not mentioned in the National Curriculum:

- the structure of the heart (ISEB Y6 2a)
- the structure of the lungs in outline only (ISEB Y6 2c)
- gas exchange in the lungs (ISEB Y6 2c)
- explaining the effect of exercise on pulse rate (ISEB Y6 2d)
- food is a fuel for respiration and a raw material for growth and repair (ISEB Y6 2h)
- how to carry out the iodine test for starch (ISEB Y6 2h)
- the roles of the skeleton, especially in movement (ISEB Y6 2i)
- how antagonistic muscle pairs move joints (ISEB Y6 2i).

Activities in this chapter offer opportunities to work scientifically by:

- taking careful measurements and looking for patterns in data
- using scientific understanding to explain patterns and to draw conclusions
- using models to help understanding.

Exercise 2.1a

1 To pump the blood around the body.

2 (a) arteries, veins and capillaries

   (b) arteries

   (c) veins

3 oxygen and glucose

4 respiration

5 carbon dioxide

6 We use more energy when exercising. Energy is released from glucose using oxygen in the cells, so the more exercise the more oxygen and glucose must be delivered to the cells by the blood. Therefore the heart has to beat faster to pump the blood around the body more quickly.

7 The blood enters the heart from the body through a vein. It is then pumped to the lungs to pick up oxygen and get rid of carbon dioxide. It then returns to the other side of the heart and is pumped out through the arteries to the rest of the body.

Exercise 2.1b

1 heart, blood

2 arteries, veins, capillaries

3 arteries

4 veins

5 oxygen

6 respiration

7 waste

8 valves

9 exercise

Exercise 2.1c: extension

Requires individual assessment. Give credit for correct science, such as route taken around the body and picking up and delivering oxygen. Also the blood plasma depositing carbon dioxide in the lungs, collecting glucose from the gut and delivering it to cells and removal of waste carbon dioxide.

Exercise 2.2

1 lungs

2 surface area

3 oxygen

4 carbon dioxide

5 quickly, oxygen

6 tar

7 exercising, oxygen

8 lung cancer, emphysema, heart attack

9 passive smoking

Exercise 2.3

1 Protects vital organs (for example, brain, heart and lungs), supports the body and allows movement.

2 antagonistic pair

3 biceps and triceps

4 To close the joint, the triceps relax and the biceps contract, pulling the lower arm up. To open the joint the biceps relax and the triceps contract, pulling the lower arm back down.

5 hinge joint

6 hip joint

Exercise 2.4a

1 The body becomes reliant on a drug and it is then hard to stop taking it.

2 nicotine

3 Alcohol affects one's ability to react quickly and may make one more likely to take risks.

4 liver

5 They may become violent, they may lose their balance, they may become sick and may be unwell the following day as the body removes the alcohol from the blood.

6 A drug that can be safely taken to cure a disease or relieve pain.

7 The dose of the medicine is worked out specifically for the person for whom it was prescribed. If taken incorrectly medicines can cause harm.

8 The syringe may contain traces of drugs and/or blood carrying diseases such as hepatitis or HIV/AIDS.

Exercise 2.4b

Requires individual assessment. Give credit for correct science.

3 Microbes

This chapter covers the following elements not mentioned in the National Curriculum:

- that micro-organisms are living organisms which are often too small to be seen and that they may be beneficial or harmful (ISEB Y6 2g)
- the discovery of antibiotics and their role in curing infections (ISEB Y6 2f)
- the role of vaccination in disease prevention (ISEB Y6 2f, 2g).

Activities in this chapter offer opportunities to work scientifically by:

- carrying out research using books and the internet
- carrying out a controlled investigation
- recognising variables
- planning a fair test.

Exercise 3.1a

1 microscopically small living thing

2 micro-organisms

3 bacteria, fungi and viruses

4 typhoid, cholera, sore throat (accept other valid answers)

5 colds, flu, measles, mumps, chicken pox (accept valid alternatives)

6 touch, through the air (e.g. sneezing) through contaminated drinking water, by animals (e.g. flies)

7 (a) John Snow

   (b) He plotted cholera cases on a map and then took the handle off the water pump in the most heavily affected area. The number of cases decreased showing that it had been the water from the pump that caused the disease.

8 Robert Koch

Exercise 3.1b

1 small, microscope

2 harmful, helpful

3 bacteria, fungi, viruses

4 bacteria

5 colds, flu

6 drinking water, air, touch

Exercise 3.2

1 Microbes on unwashed hands get into the mouth and then may cause disease.

2 after using the toilet, after handling animals, after playing outdoors, before meals

3 Sneeze and/or wipe your nose on a tissue and then dispose of the tissue. Put your hand in front of our mouth when coughing. Wash hands frequently.

4 (a) antibiotics

   (b) Alexander Fleming left a dish used to study bacteria unwashed. After a while he discovered that a mould had grown on it and that the mould seemed to be killing the bacteria.

   (c) Colds and flu are caused by viruses and these are not killed by antibiotics.

5 They put a small amount of the virus into your body and this encourages the immune system to produce antibodies. These will then recognise the disease and fight it off if it enters the body again.

Exercise 3.3a

1 Gloucestershire

2 smallpox

3 milkmaids, cowpox

4 fluid

5 smallpox

6 children

7 vaccination

8 extinct

Exercise 3.3b: extension

This will need individual assessment. Give credit for understanding of the viewpoint of the chosen character and for telling the story accurately.

Exercise 3.4

1 bread, cheese, yoghurt, chocolate (accept other valid suggestions)

2 They break down waste in the environment and return nutrients to the soil.

3 They help to digest food and release nutrients, boost the immune system, keep the digestive system healthy and help to fight harmful bacteria in the gut.

4 (a) yeast

(b) It carries out respiration and releases carbon dioxide. This gets trapped as bubbles in the dough.

5 unleavened bread

6 The action of yeast on sugars to produce alcohol.

7 Yeast is added to fruit juice to ferment the sugars.

8 The drinking water was unsafe but the fermentation process kills bacteria and so wine and beer were safer to drink than the water.

4 Evolution and inheritance

This chapter covers the following elements of the National Curriculum for Year 6.

Pupils should be taught to:

- recognise that living things have changed over time and that fossils provide information about living things that inhabited the Earth millions of years ago
- recognise that living things produce offspring of the same kind, but normally offspring vary and are not identical to their parents
- identify how animals and plants are adapted to suit their environment in different ways and that adaptation may lead to evolution.

Activities in this chapter offer opportunities to work scientifically by:

- considering how the work of scientists over time contributes to our current understanding and that there is always more to discover
- using a variety of sources to research and present information.

Exercise 4.1a

1 palaeontologist

2 A dead animal or plant falls to the bottom of the sea and rapidly becomes covered in sediment. As more sediment builds up over the remains the pressure and minerals seeping in from the surrounding sediment turn the remains of the plant or animal to rock.

3 Sea creatures, especially those with shells because land organisms are less likely to get covered in sediment quickly enough and the hard parts are more likely to survive than soft tissue.

4 coal

5 warm swampy forests

6 No. They can tell us something about the body structure but only very rarely are the soft parts preserved and the colour cannot be identified by observation. (Modern DNA analysis has recently given some clues about the colour of a few extraordinarily well-preserved specimens.)

Exercise 4.1b

1 animal, sediment

2 shells, bones

3 palaeontologists, clues, details

4 coal

Exercise 4.1c: extension

Soft silty ground is most likely because the tracks are clear and the animal obviously sank into the surface quite deeply.

Exercise 4.2a

1 terrible lizard

2 reptiles

3 Tyrannosaurus

4 bones/skeleton

5 Because a few fossils show traces of the scaly skin covering. Also they can guess that they might be similar to today's reptiles.

6 It was the first dinosaur to be found to have had feathers and it forms a link between dinosaurs and modern birds.

7 Cretaceous

8 at the end of the Jurassic

9 65 million years ago

10 an asteroid strike

Exercise 4.2b

1 lizard, Greek

2 millions

3 Triceratops

4 colour

5 Triassic

6 Cretaceous

7 asteroid

Exercise 4.2c: extension

These animals were not alive at the same time and most of them lived in the Cretaceous period not the Jurassic.

Exercise 4.3

1 Lyme Regis, Dorset, in 1799

2 It was famous for all the fossils found there.

3 To sell to collectors to earn money to support her family.

4 She carefully chipped away the rock surrounding them and cleaned them up so they could be clearly seen.

5 Ichthyosaurus

6 William Bullock's Museum of Natural Curiosities in London

7 Plesiosaurus and Pterodactylus

8 They helped people to understand the age of the Earth and the history of life on Earth.

9 In a stained glass window in the local church.

Exercise 4.4a

1 a gradual change in a species of animal or plant over time

2 (a) HMS Beagle

(b) Captain FitzRoy

(c) His job was as companion and assistant to Captain FitzRoy. He also documented the animal and plant species found in the various places they visited.

3 Galapagos

4 Each island had species of animals and birds (especially tortoises and finches) that looked similar but were slightly different on each island.

5 (a) As all individuals are slightly different some will be better than others at surviving in a given set of conditions. These are more likely to breed and their offspring are likely to inherit the favourable characteristics. Over time these characteristics become more and more common in the population.

(b) natural selection

6 They didn't like the fact that it caused people to question the Biblical account and some did not like being told that they were descended from monkeys.

7 (a) Alfred Russel Wallace

(b) Indonesia

8 Through continued discovery of new fossils and using genetics.

Exercise 4.4b

In the past some individuals in a population of an ancestor of the giraffe might have had longer necks. This made them able to reach leaves higher on the trees and therefore they would be better fed and stronger than the others. These stronger individuals would be likely to mate with each other and some or all of their offspring would have longer necks. Over many generations the necks would get progressively longer until they reached the length they are in modern giraffes.

Exercise 4.5

1 wolf

2 Selective breeding is when people select plants or animals with desirable characteristics to breed from. Their offspring are more likely to have these characteristics and the best of these would be chosen to breed from in the next generation, and their offspring would be even more likely to show the selected characteristics. Over many generations a new improved variety is created.

3 Selective breeding has produced varieties of plants and animals that provide us with greater quantities of better quality food. This allows more children to survive, so increasing populations. More food can be produced from smaller areas, making it possible for more people to live in one place and leading to the development of larger societies, towns and cities. Give credit for any sensible suggestion showing understanding that improved crops and farm animals make it easier for people to feed themselves.

5 Hot and cold

This chapter covers the following elements of the ISEB syllabus for Year 6.

Pupils should be taught that:

● some materials are better thermal insulators than others (ISEB Y6 4a)
● temperature is a measure of how hot or cold things are (ISEB Y6 4b).

Exercise 5.1

1 Hero

2 Floating glass spheres that floated or sank according to the temperature.

3 no universally accepted scale

4 expand: get larger
   contract: get smaller

5 mercury

6 boiling: 212°F
   freezing: 32°F

7 oven, fridge/freezer, medical (taking body temperature) (accept valid alternatives)

8 Cannot line up the top of the liquid with the scale accurately unless eye is at the same level.

Exercise 5.2a

1 trap air

2 loft: prevents thermal energy escaping through roof

   windows: double glazing and curtains trap layer of air to stop thermal energy escaping through windows

   cavity walls: stops thermal energy being lost through walls

3 fluff up their fur/feathers

4 The vacuum surrounding the inner flask and the layer of trapped air between inner and outer flask stops thermal energy passing through from hot drink to cooler air.

Exercise 5.2b

1 warm, pumped

2 thermal

3 thermal, insulation

4 air

5 fluffy

Exercise 5.2c: extension

Individual exercises need assessing on the accuracy of the information, clarity of writing with regard to target audience, presentation, sources of information, images, etc.

Exercise 5.3

1 carbon dioxide, methane

2 Stop some of the thermal energy from escaping into space, keeping temperatures relatively stable.

3 Increase in greenhouse gases leading to more thermal energy being trapped.

4 Reduce electricity use, walk or cycle instead of driving, use local resources, reuse or recycle as much as possible (accept valid alternatives).

Exercise 5.4a

1 Metal is a good thermal conductor so a metal knife allows thermal energy to flow out of your hand. A woolly scarf is a thermal insulator so prevents thermal energy from flowing away.

2 Responses should include clear description of shape, mention of material used for body of pan and handle with explanation for choices.

Exercise 5.4b

1 insulator

2 conductor

3 saucepan, conductor, metal

4 thermal, plastic

Exercise 5.4c: extension

1 Snowflakes trap air, so although snow is cold it is quite a good thermal insulator and will trap enough thermal energy to keep people warm enough to survive until rescued.

2 Layer of trapped air prevents thermal energy from hotter air flowing into cooler body. / Flow of air around body can move excess thermal energy away.

6 Indicators

Exercise 6.1a

1 A material used to show the presence or absence of a substance, usually by a change of colour.

2 pink

3 The liquid is an alkali.

4 Not very — indicates presence of acid with a strong colour change but does not distinguish well between neutral and alkaline substances.

5 Acids and alkalis are corrosive and can easily cause damage to eyes.

6 fruit juices, especially citrus fruits, vinegar

Exercise 6.1b

Liquids may be acids, alkalis or NEUTRAL substances. Acids and alkalis are both CORROSIVE so it is important to wear EYE protection when using them in the lab. An example of a safe acid found in the kitchen is VINEGAR/LEMON JUICE/OTHER FRUIT JUICES.

An indicator is a substance that changes COLOUR in acids and alkalis. Litmus is an indicator that is PINK in acid and BLUE in alkali.

Light and sight

This chapter covers the following elements of the National Curriculum for Year 6.

Pupils should be taught to:

- recognise that light appears to travel in straight lines
- use the idea that light travels in straight lines to explain that objects are seen because they give out or reflect light into the eye
- explain that we see things because light travels from light sources to our eyes or from light sources to objects and then to our eyes
- use the idea that light travels in straight lines to explain why shadows have the same shape as the objects that cast them.

It also includes the following elements not mentioned in the National Curriculum:

- how light is reflected at plane surfaces (ISEB Y6 5a)
- measurement of angles of incidence and reflection (ISEB Y6 5a)
- the Law of Reflection (ISEB Y6 5a)
- that non-luminous objects are seen because light scattered from them enters the eye (ISEB Y6 5d).

Activities in this chapter offer opportunities to work scientifically by:

- carrying out measurements accurately using appropriate equipment
- using observations and measurements to identify patterns in data and draw conclusions
- communicating ideas clearly and evaluating the accuracy of explanations
- using clearly drawn diagrams to illustrate concepts.

Exercise 7.1

1 luminous

2 opaque

3 opaque, blocks

4 straight

5 same, different

Exercise 7.2a

1 (a) bounced back

   (b) taken in

2 Mirrors have very smooth shiny surfaces so the light rays are not scattered at the surface.

3

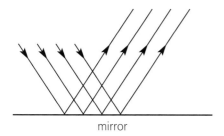

mirror

4 The light rays are all reflected/scattered in different directions.

5 No. The image will be the same shape and colour as the original but will be back-to-front.

Exercise 7.2b

1 reflected

2 smooth

3 scatter

4 plane

Exercise 7.2c: extension

1 red, orange, yellow, green, blue, indigo, violet

2 It was already known that white light passing through a prism came out in the colours of the spectrum, but it was believed that the prism was adding colour to the light. Newton showed that a second prism placed in the path of the coloured light could be made to turn the light back to white, thus proving that the prism was splitting the light rather than colouring it.

Exercise 7.3

1 the incident ray

2 the normal

3 the angle of incidence equals the angle of reflection

4 C

5 The diagram should show the normal, the angle of incidence and the angle of reflection correctly drawn with all angles accurately measured.

Exercise 7.4a

1 luminous

2 light

3 eyelid

4 iris

5 pupil

6   lens

7   retina, brain

8   compound

9   spiders

10   light and dark

Exercise 7.4b: extension

1   Rods detect light and dark. Cones detect colour (red, green and blue).

2   Give credit for any well-researched facts about animal eyesight – e.g. colour range, ability to detect infrared or ultraviolet, ability to see in very low light levels, sight lost by animals in dark environment.

Exercise 7.5a

1   Luminous objects give out light but non-luminous objects do not create light of their own.

2   **(a)**   We see luminous objects when light rays coming from them travel (in straight lines) into our eyes.

(b)   Diagram should show light ray, with arrow, travelling from a luminous object, e.g. candle, straight to the eye.

3   **(a)**   We see non-luminous objects when light is reflected from them and travels (in straight lines) into our eyes.

(b)   Diagram should show light ray from a luminous source, e.g. lamp or Sun, shining onto a non-luminous object and being reflected into the eye. The incident ray and the reflected ray should be continuous not separated at the reflecting surface. For example:

4 Light rays travel in straight lines. A building is opaque (usually) so light from an object round a corner cannot pass through the building in a straight line, nor can it bend at the corner to reach our eyes.

5 The diagram should show a mirror correctly placed at the corner and a light ray from a luminous object (or reflected by a non-luminous object) being reflected at the mirror into the eye of the observer. For example:

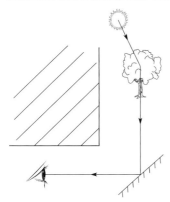

Exercise 7.5b

1 Any two luminous objects (e.g. Sun, lamp, torch, fire). Could also include examples of bioluminescence (e.g. some jellyfish, fireflies, glow worms).

2 Any two objects that are not luminous (e.g. book, table). Some may realise that a torch or a candle are not luminous if not switched on/lit. Some may include the Moon and planets.

3 Answer should include a luminous object with a correctly drawn ray of light travelling from the luminous object to the eye of the observer. For example:

4 Answer should include a non-luminous object and a light source with a ray of light from the light source falling onto the object and being reflected into the eye of the observer. For example:

8 Changing electrical circuits

This chapter covers the following elements of the National Curriculum for Year 6.

Pupils should be taught to:

- associate the brightness of a lamp or the volume of a buzzer with the number and voltage of the cells used in the circuit
- compare and give reasons for variations in how components function, including the brightness of bulbs, the loudness of buzzers and the on/off position of switches
- use recognised symbols when representing a simple circuit in a diagram.

It also includes the following elements not mentioned in the National Curriculum:

- history of making electricity
- how to recognise a short circuit and the safety implications of short circuits (ISEB Y6 6c).

Activities in this chapter offer opportunities to work scientifically by:

- comparing circuits and explaining similarities and differences
- applying knowledge of electrical components and the working of circuits to create circuits to fulfil a particular function
- showing understanding of and attention to health and safety issues connected with electricity.

Exercise 8.1a

1 It needs to be made to flow in a controlled way around a circuit.

2 Alessandro Volta

3 A pile of metal plates with wet card in between.

4 Joseph Swan and Thomas Edison

5 Michael Faraday

6 New York

7 fossil fuels

8 They release carbon dioxide (a greenhouse gas) and other harmful gases when burnt.

9 Accept any three appropriate suggestions.

10 Accept any two appropriate suggestions.

Exercise 8.1b

1 Galvani attached wires to the nerves in legs from frogs and passed the electricity from lightning through them. The muscles in the legs twitched when the electricity flowed through, showing that messages passing through the nerves to the muscles are electrical.

2 He obtained the electricity from lightning strikes which contain far more energy than mains circuits and so it was very dangerous.

3 *Frankenstein* by Mary Shelley.

Exercise 8.2a

1 (a)

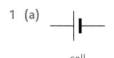

cell

(b)

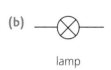

lamp

(c)

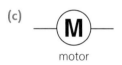

motor

(d)

open switch

(e)

buzzer

2 (a)

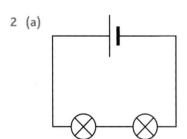

(b) Less than normal brightness/half normal brightness because the energy from one cell is shared between the two lamps.

3

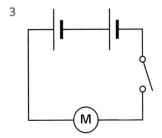

Exercise 8.2b: extension

This will need assessing as appropriate, giving credit for scientific accuracy, imagination, clarity of writing and presentation.